IN SEARCH OF A PERFECT FATHER

THE BEAUTY OF THE DOCTRINE OF GOD

ALED SEAGO

The Latimer Trust

In Search of a Perfect Father: The Beauty of the Doctrine of God © Aled Seago 2023. All rights reserved.
ISBN 978-1-916834-01-9 Published by the Latimer Trust February 2024.

The Latimer Trust (formerly Latimer House, Oxford) is a conservative Evangelical research organisation within the Church of England, whose main aim is to promote the history and theology of Anglicanism as understood by those in the Reformed tradition. Interested readers are welcome to consult its website for further details of its many activities.

The Latimer Trust
London N14 4PS UK
Registered Charity: 1084337
Company Number: 4104465
www.latimertrust.org
administrator@latimertrust.org

Views expressed in works published by The Latimer Trust are those of the authors and do not necessarily represent the official position of The Latimer Trust.

The honesty with which Aled writes is humbling. He takes difficult truths revealed in Scripture and brings them to the reader with clear and simple explanations. I was moved by the way in which Aled sought to apply this doctrine to the life and experience of the Christian so that the Fatherly goodness of God might be known, appreciated and cherished. Thank you, Aled.

> Helen Baker, Distinctive Deacon at St. John's
> Knutsford and Toft

Aled has written an accessible introduction to classical theism. With pastoral warmth he focusses on the otherness of God, seeking to show how meditation on the creator-creature distinction can bring us a greater sense of security and comfort in Him, especially during the toughest challenges of life.

> Sophie Bannister, Assistant Minister, St John the
> Baptist, Spalding

This little book is like a deep dive into a warm bath! Our ultimate purpose and greatest joy is to know God as our loving Father. Aled helps us grasp the wonder and the beauty of God's infinite perfection personally. Not only does he make the majesty of God accessible, he also show what it means and how much it means. Here is rich truth for real life with honesty, depth, warmth and humour.

> George Crowder, Regional Director, Church Society
> and Vicar, St John's Over

Contents Page

Foreword to the Christian Doctrine Series	1
Acknowledgements	5
Introduction	7
1. God is... A Wrong Story of God?	9
2. God as Creator	11
3. God as Father	49
Final Reflection: Will I Let God Disagree With Me?	59
Permissions	63
Bibliography and Further Reading	65

Foreword to the Christian Doctrine Series

What does the Anglican Church teach? What should Anglicans believe? The Anglican Communion has a reputation for tolerating a wide variety of different viewpoints, so much so that it is easy to forget that there is a core of teaching, or doctrine, which Anglicans are expected to teach and believe. Most of that core is shared with other Christians to a greater or lesser extent, but there is often a distinctive way in which Anglicans relate to that common heritage and adapt it for their own mission as witnesses to Jesus Christ in the world.

There are many good studies of Anglican doctrine available, and some of them give detailed accounts for the benefit of students and theologians from other churches. Unfortunately, there is relatively little material that addresses the needs and concerns of ordinary churchgoers, many of whom have only a sketchy awareness of the Church's teaching and are baffled by an academic approach and technical terminology that they find hard to understand. The aim of this series is to present the doctrine of the Anglican Church, and in particular of the Church of England, in a format that is user friendly and that does not assume any prior knowledge of the subject. It cannot be exhaustive, but it aims to be reasonably comprehensive and to give readers a clear sense of what the Anglican Church stands for.

Anglicans do not claim to be a special kind of Christians, distinguished from others by peculiar beliefs that set them apart from the wider Christian world. On the contrary, Anglicans claim that what we believe is 'basic

Christianity' as the late John Stott put it in a book that he wrote on the subject, or 'mere Christianity' as C. S. Lewis described it in a similar volume. Anglicans adhere to the mainstream of Christian belief as this has been handed down through the centuries, and members of other Churches will find much in our heritage with which they can agree. That is as it should be, and we hope that where we take a different position to that of some other Christians, that we do so in a spirit of love and respect for them and their witness alongside our own.

In the course of time, Anglicans have rejected what they regard as aberrations in the teachings of some other Churches, and especially of the Roman Catholic Church, from which we separated at the time of the Reformation in the sixteenth century. We think that some of their doctrines have obscured the pure message of Christ and imposed beliefs that have no basis in the Bible, which is the supreme source of our faith. On other matters of controversy among Christians, Anglicans have either taken a moderate position that has tried to reconcile differences as much as possible, or else has remained silent, allowing Church members the freedom to have their own opinions without making them part of its essential beliefs. The booklets in this Series will deal with these questions and explain why Anglicans think the way they do, without condemning or dismissing the views of those who differ from us on questions where views other than our own can be defended from the Holy Scriptures that we share in common.

The aim of this Series is to guide readers through the various aspects of the Church's doctrine, avoiding technical terms as much as possible, and explaining them clearly when that is necessary. Readers who want to pursue particular subjects further are provided with a list of publications that will help them deepen their knowledge and understanding.

It is the hope of the Latimer Trust that this Series will awaken an interest among Church members in Christian beliefs that will stimulate their minds and help them grow in their faith. The Series aims to lay a foundation for the vital task of explaining what Anglicans teach and believe in a way that can be communicated positively and accurately to the wider world. It is our hope that preachers and pastors will find in it a clear presentation of the message of Jesus Christ that will guide them in their ministerial task as they proclaim the Good News of salvation to their people. May God bless them as they labour for him, and may he use the tools this Series provides for his glory and for the upbuilding of his Church.

Gerald Bray
Series Editor

Acknowledgements

To my friend, former boss and minister George Crowder. Thank you for being such a source of encouragement as a pastor, friend and brother, and for first introducing me to this wonderful subject.

To my former college principal, doctrine teacher, fellow Anglican, friend and brother, Mike Ovey (1958–2017). I would not be where I am today without him. Mike taught me Doctrine of God at Oak Hill, as well as modelling a humble awe of God. His death forced us all to confront the truth he always taught us: that God is God, and we are not.

To good and supportive friends: Ian and Jodi Chidlow, Suzanne Sherrat and Catherine Cleghorn.

I am grateful too to the inaugural members of the first Growing in Christ doctrine course I ran at St George's Poynton in 2020, where some of this material was tested and refined. So, thanks to Sarah Williams, Dave and Hannah Brackenbury, and Bizzy Bowles.

To all staff and pupils at Altrincham Church of England Primary School for their kind support.

To my wife Jo – a reminder of God's merciful grace. Thank you for your love, your patience and your hilarity.

For my godchildren Evie-Beth and George. May there never be a day when you do not know this God.

Introduction

*'You are worthy, our Lord and God,
to receive glory and honour and
power, for you created all things,
and by your will they were created
and have their being.'*
Revelation 4:11

In my first months as a curate in the Church of England, our church studied the book of Job. One striking thing about the book is how God responds to Job. After many, many cycles of speeches, where bad theology leads to bad comfort, God speaks.

He does not answer the questions Job has. Instead, he speaks about *himself*. The theological journey Job goes through involves expanding his perception of God. What I find striking here is that the response to suffering given to Job is an exposition of the nature and character of God himself. What Job needed to hear in his confused and unexpected suffering was that God is never confused, he is never surprised, and he is always good. The character of God was used by God himself to counsel Job. Job is a book about the nature of God in the context of unexplained and unexpected suffering.

The doctrine of God is what the Bible and the church teach concerning the character and nature of God. Far from over-philosophising or putting the uncontainable God in a box, this doctrine is clear and compelling. When life gets hard, what we believe or do not believe about God becomes of central concern to us.

For those who have grown up in unloving or abusive homes, the doctrine of God – as Creator and as Father

– is particularly precious. No one has a perfect father. The best and worst of dads pale in comparison to the goodness of God as Father. Many people grieve that their relationship with their own father is not what they wish it had been. Since that is true for me, I have found myself returning again and again to this particular aspect of the doctrine of God. The truth of the Fatherhood of God occupies a special place in my heart and is a huge daily comfort.

Our view of God is often far too small. As Matthew Barrett notes, God has become for many of us, 'domesticated.'[1] But God is fundamentally *not* like us – and that is the best news for anyone who faces depression like me. *God is God, and I am not.* This simple sentence has huge intellectual and pastoral implications.

We will aim to unpack some of those pastoral implications together. We will consider what we mean by calling God 'Father' and 'Creator' and we will aim to make this doctrine real in our hearts and lives.[2]

---

[1] See generally Matthew Barrett, *None Greater: The Undomesticated Attributes of God* (Grand Rapids, MI.: Baker Books, 2019).
[2] By 'we' I am chiefly drawing on and referring to the Bible and the formularies of the Anglican church.

God is... A Wrong Story of God?

Steve Chalke, a former evangelical minister, caused attention some years ago by commenting that adhering to certain traditional doctrines of the Bible and Church of England was 'telling the wrong story about God.'[1] According to him, those who confessed that they believed Jesus' death on the cross took our deserved punishment, in our place, and appeased God's wrath, were telling an abhorrent story, one that is not true of God at all.

This is not the place to discuss the issues Chalke had with the penal, substitutionary atonement of Christ, since that is not the subject of this work. What it is worthy of note though is the reasons for Chalke's issue. They are not primarily intellectual, but pastoral. In other words, a classically confessed doctrine is seen as wrong, partially because of the *pastoral implications*.

This matters as we talk about God. Our experiences, whether our own or other people's, can draw us towards or away from certain doctrines. A lot of the 'classical' tenets of the doctrine of God are debated, and indeed often rejected, because of what appear to be unhelpful pastoral implications. Particularly concerning for some people are questions regarding God's familiarity, his sovereignty and the problem of evil. Of course, we do not want to say that God is completely unfamiliar, nor are we dismissing the valid questions concerning

---

[1] Steve Chalke, symposium at the London School of Theology, July 2005. Cited by Michael J. Ovey in 'Off the Record: Is the Wrath of God Extremist?' in Chris Green (ed.), *The Goldilocks Zone: The Collected Writings of Michael J. Ovey* (Nottingham, IVP, 2018), 80.

sovereignty and evil. What we are saying is that we must take care when investigating these doctrines, and not just from an intellectual point of view.

In order to understand the implications of this doctrine, we are discussing two fundamental aspects of who God is. He is Creator, and he is Father.

God as Creator

> 'Who is Aslan? Do you know him?' 'Well, he knows me,' said Edmund.
> *Voyage of the Dawn Treader,*
> C S Lewis.

God is God, I am not.

That short sentence may be the most important one in this book.

Obvious? Of course. Easily forgotten? Yes.

God, by nature of being God, is different from us in various ways. In fact, God is so different from us, he is entirely 'other'. It is not as if God is like us, but stronger. No, we cannot accurately describe what he is like. His nature is foreign to us. Does this mean that he is completely unknowable? Can we relate to a God who is entirely other? Our answer is that God is sufficiently knowable, but not exhaustively so. We can know *enough* about God to meet our needs, without knowing *everything* about him. So, while God is not limited like we are, he is also relatable, and relational, in a way that is sufficient for us.

The most reliable testimony concerning God is from God himself. Just as I am the most reliable testimony if you wanted to know things about me, God's divine self-revelation is trustworthy. It is, of course, much more trustworthy than I am. Psalm 19 (and other places) testifies that the Bible, God's word, is his divine self-revelation. The purpose of the Bible is revealing an unknown, yet knowable God. The other dynamic at work here is that God is Father. God is Father, because he has a Son. This Son, Jesus, is fully human and fully divine. Therefore, he makes the unknown known. Part of the reason Jesus became incarnate, as well as to make atonement for our sins, was to make the otherness of God known to us finite creatures.

Pause and let that sink in for just a moment. God is knowable, but not on our terms. He is too big for us to know – unless he reveals himself. For God to be knowable, he must be the one who makes himself known. And that is good news! God's revelation is *of himself, from himself, to us*. We can know God because he speaks to us concerning himself, in a way we can understand.

The Creator-Creature distinction

Our task at hand is not to boil down God to a basic definable point, because that is impossible. We cannot put God in a box. God is not just a bigger version of us, a spiritual strongman who can swoop in and sort out the mess. He is *Creator*. We are not creators in that sense. We are creatures, created for a relationship with God our Creator, as well as one another as fellow creatures. This distinction between Creator and creature is fundamental to understanding who God is, who we are, and how we are to live.

God is our Creator.

We are his creatures.

In other words, *God is God, and I am not*. This is the root of the Creator-Creature distinction. *God is different.* We are not God, nor will we ever be. Grasping this key point of God's 'otherness' is vital. The essence of sin is to blur this Creator-Creature distinction: either by trying to reduce God to our level or by presuming to elevate ourselves to his.

Consider J R R Tolkien. He is most famous for his works set in Middle Earth: *The Hobbit and The Lord of the Rings.* Tolkien, as a Christian, did not set out to write an allegory of the Christian faith, yet his theist world view comes across on every page. If you dip into Tolkien's *The Silmarillion,* designed as a history of Middle Earth, you will note not just the historical context, but the theological one as well. Middle Earth is created by one God, who is its Father. His creation rebels against him, because in their pride they wish to be creators. That occurs time and time again – and eventually will play out in Sauron's crafting of the One Ring and attempt to subdue all Middle Earth under his divine rule. Time and time again, Tolkien's works reflect the desire we all have to blur the Creator-Creature distinction.

This Creator-Creature distinction means that we cannot know God in the way he knows himself, because we are his creatures. We can only know things within the limits of what we are. My dog is very clever, but there are certain things he cannot know, because his nature restricts him, and so it is with us.

We are not God; we have limits. That is not a popular thing to say in Western culture, yet, establishing this point of humble knowing is vital if we wish to delve into the mysteries of God.

Humble knowing is not the same as self-hatred. Self-hatred is just as toxic as disordered self-love. Humble knowing is an acceptance of our creaturely status before our Creator God.[1] To start with this humility, we have two fundamental concepts to guide us:

- God knows himself *fully*
- We know God *sufficiently*

We cannot know *everything* about God. There is much we do not know. Only God has this perfect self-knowledge. But the good news is we can know *enough* about our great big God. Enough to make us realise who God is, what he has done, and why he is worthy of our worship. We can only know about God what he has revealed to us about himself. We define God on his terms, and not ours. We know God truly, but not exhaustively.[2]

So, what do we know of God, concerning his status as our Creator? There are things that God is, that we can never be. His otherness means that he exhibits attributes we do not, as well as ones we do.

The attributes of God

Attributes are characteristics of God. As we will see, they are not parts that make up the whole of God. He is not a jigsaw of parts. Rather, they are characteristics that he always exhibits in equal measure. There are two types of divine attributes: *communicable* attributes and *incommunicable* attributes.

---

[1] The best book I have ever read on this point is Tim Keller's *The Freedom of Self Forgetfulness* (Chorley: 10 Publishing, 2012). Get it!

[2] Michael J. Ovey, 'Is God the Only Theologian?' in Richard Cunningham (ed.), *Serving the Church, Reaching the World: Essays in Honour of Don Carson* (Nottingham: IVP, 2017).

Communicable attributes are facts about God that we can understand or share. For example, 'love' is a communicable attribute. We love, as God's image bearers. He defines love, and we know something of what love is like. Other examples are anger and truth. We know what they mean, because there is an image of those attributes (however flawed) in us.

Incommunicable attributes are facts about God that we do not share with him, and we find extremely difficult to understand. They are attributes he has as Creator that are impossible for us to have as creatures; they will not be shared with us. These attributes are so alien to us that God must communicate them in a way that we can understand. To use the language of John Calvin, it is as if God is 'lisping' to us.

If you have children, have taught children, or even interacted with children, you will know that we have to break down complex ideas into words they will understand when we are talking to them. A five-year-old once asked me in a Sunday school setting to define pride. I could have said: 'disordered self-love and nauseating narcissism.' That would not have helped! Instead, I had to say: 'It's when you think you are better than everyone else, and it is not very nice.' The fact she was actually talking about a group of lions was ... well, unfortunate!

These incommunicable attributes are essential to God's 'Godness,' and are attested to in Scripture. Although some of the terms we might use are not necessarily mentioned in the Bible, the ideas most certainly are. We will examine seven attributes in turn and attempt an understanding of what they mean, and how they are communicated. However, before we do so we need to take note of the foundation that undergirds these attributes: God is perfect, and God is one.

1. God is the perfect promise keeper

We are examining how God, because he is Creator, is not like us. Foundational to God's otherness is that he is the perfect promise keeper in Scripture.[3] The whole story of the Bible is the story of the relationship between God and his people, based on his word.[4]

In other words, God's promise, and its fulfilment in the person and work of Jesus Christ, the Spirit-filled Son sent by the Father, is the centre of the Bible. God is a God of relationships, and these relationships are based on his word: his promise, his covenant.

For that to be so, God needs to keep the promises he makes, and because he is God, he does so perfectly. To be able to be that perfect promise-keeping God, God must not be limited like we are as creatures. If God is uncreated, he is not bound by anything, except by his perfect moral character.

There is nothing capable of reining God in, because he made everything. He is worthy of all worship: glory, honour and power, *because* he is the uncreated Creator.

---

[3] With gratitude to Mike Ovey for his Doctrine of God lectures at Oak Hill Theological College, September 2016. The whole module flowed out of this idea. 'Get your ideas around that,' Mike said to us, 'and everything else will follow.'
[4] I am grateful to Rev George Crowder, who coined this phrase when we preached through a Bible Overview sermon series together at St John's Over in Winsford, UK, in the summer of 2014.

We *need* God to be perfect for him to be able to keep his promises. In other words, God is *unimprovable*. He is not like the latest smartphone that will only be the latest smartphone for about twelve months before an upgrade. God is at his maximum, always has been, and always will be. This is expressed very well in a piece of liturgy from the Anglican Church in Uganda:

> God is good. All the time.
> And all the time, God is good, and that is his nature.
> Wow!

2. *God is simple*

Having established God is different from us by being perfect, we need to ask the extent of his perfection. Is it only in part, or the whole? This brings us to what is known as the doctrine of simplicity.

We have seen that God is God, and I am not. *God is the perfect promise keeper.* God is different. He is not like me. He is unimprovable, and he is consistent. God's 'simplicity' means that he is not made up of different parts. As C S Lewis explained in *Out of the Silent Planet:*

> It became plain that [God] was a spirit without body, parts or passions.

Whole books could be, and have been, written concerning this – but we can only deal with it briefly here. It is well worth looking at other works which go into greater depth.[5]

---

[5] In particular, see James E. Dolezal's *All That is in God: Evangelical Theology and the Challenge of Classic Christian*

Perhaps this term 'simplicity' surprises you? When you started thinking about the nature of God, was the last word you were looking for 'simple?' If anything, studying God is complicated! The word 'simple' in this context does not refer to simple rather than complicated, but simple as opposed to complex.

We can talk of shopping centres as 'complex'. They are large buildings, made up of many different shops. Within each of them is a selection of large and small shops, with a variety of brands and products on sale. In other words, they all occupy different spaces and sell different things inside one shopping centre; but they are parts of the whole. In fact, another word for a shopping centre is 'complex' – not because a shopping centre is complicated, but because it is made of different parts. A shopping centre is never simple, because it has lots of different shops, and therefore it is complex.[6]

We are 'complex' beings in the sense that we have different roles; there are certain things that need to be in place to show who we are. I am a vicar – which is quite a large part of who I am. Yet I was not always a vicar, nor will I always be one. I am also a husband, but again that is an additional part of me that began one day, and will one day go.

God is not complex in that sense. He is not built of parts that make up his essence. He's not like a jigsaw with many different pieces that build a picture. He is not made up of bits. He is not a mosaic, nor a bunch of separate ingredients that come together as God. We

---

Theism (Grand Rapids, MI.: Reformed Heritage Books, 2017).
6   I'm grateful to fellow college student Robbie Strachan for this helpful illustration.

cannot construct God out of principal parts. Instead, we confess that *he is one.*

Many of the historic Christian confessions and creeds put it in terms of God being 'without body, parts or passions.' This is stated in Article 1 of the Thirty-Nine Articles of the Church of England:

> There is but one living and true God, everlasting, without body, parts, or passions; of infinite power, wisdom, and goodness; the Maker, and Preserver of all things both visible and invisible. And in unity of this Godhead there be three Persons, of one substance, power, and eternity; the Father, the Son, and the Holy Ghost.[7]

God *is*. There is no more to him than that.

Scripture affirms for us that: 'God is love. Whoever lives in love lives in God, and God in them' (1 John 4:16). God *is* love; he defines love. He is not *just* love, *only* love, or even *predominantly* love. He is love.

He is wrath. He is mercy. He is just. These attributes are not complex parts, like a shop of love or shop of anger in the shopping complex of God. He is *all of these* things *at the same time.*

As Katherin Rodgers explains: 'The classic tradition holds that as absolute source God is indeed Wisdom and Justice and Goodness *per se,* and other things possess these qualities through participation in the

---

[7] These articles were put together during the Reformation and are still technically the official doctrine of the Church of England. They are gold dust – definitely worth a read.

divine.'[8] Simplicity means that God is *pure act*. In other word, God is what he does. Consider how he reveals his name to Moses in Exodus 3:14, 'God said to Moses, "I AM WHO I AM."'

I AM WHO I AM is the Hebrew word, YHWH, or Yahweh. It means God is what God does. For example, in the *Mr Men* and *Little Miss* children's books, the characters' names are what they do: Mr Bounce jumps around and Little Miss Sunshine is very cheerful. God is his action. He could be, for example, Mr Creator or Mr Redeemer. When we say God is *pure act,* this is what we mean. He is always how he is.

As John of Damascus wrote:

> We, therefore, both know and confess that God is without beginning, without end, eternal and everlasting, uncreate, unchangeable, invariable, simple, uncompound, incorporeal, invisible, impalpable, uncircumscribed, infinite, incognisable, indefinable, incomprehensible, good, just, maker of all things created, almighty, all-ruling, all-surveying, of all overseer, sovereign, judge; and that God is One, that is to say, one essence.[9]

These aspects of God's character are not in competition with each other. God is not 'anger' one minute and 'love' the next. He is both, at the same time. There is

---

[8] Katherin Rodgers, *Perfect Being Theology* (Edinburgh: Edinburgh University Press, 2000), 27.
[9] In 'Exposition of the Orthodox Faith by John of Damascus.' *Church Fathers*. Kindle Locations 576609–576612.

no contradiction.

God is a single whole, not a mosaic of parts. That is a good and necessary implication of him being perfect. It means there is no chance he will compromise his character or choose to reveal a different side of it. Otherwise, how would we know that he will keep his promises?

God is not a jigsaw of competing characteristics and emotions, but is simple, *without* parts or passions. He is therefore the constantly consistent and compassionate God.

With the doctrine of simplicity, it is key to remember that it is not a complicated theory made up by boring academics. Though you will not find the term used in the Bible, you will find the ideas behind it everywhere. Remember Jesus' words in Mark 12:29, where he echoes Deuteronomy 6, which reads:

> Hear, O Israel: the LORD our God, the LORD is one. Love the LORD your God with all your heart and with all your soul and with all your strength. (Deuteronomy 6:4–5)

God is love and, at the same time, God is wrath. For us, these are highly charged emotions and ones that may conflict with each other. It is hard for us to switch from one to the other, especially if we are teenagers.

Thankfully, it does not work like that with God. God is perfect, and in control. His simplicity means that none of his attributes compete with or contradict each other. He is not fickle, or reactive, but always proactive. There is harmony, there is simplicity – 'no parts', 'no passions'.[10]

God's simplicity also means that everything about him is necessary. There are no extra features. God does not operate on bolt-ons. (When my phone runs out of data, then I must add more, which is called a bolt on.) But God is *unimprovable*.

Mike Ovey wrote that the example *par excellence* of God's simplicity is seen in the cross of Jesus Christ: 'The cross is a case ... where several attributes are simultaneously perfectly satisfied, notably justice and mercy meet.'[11] Note too the words of Psalm 85:10, where righteousness and peace kiss each other.[12] Or the words in the song, 'Come and See':

> We worship at your feet, where wrath and mercy meet.[13]

A simple God is a ruling God, because there is no compromise or competition. A simple God is a sovereign God. He is just, and he is merciful. No one attribute overrules another, for God is simple. As C S Lewis put it in his wonderful novel *Perelandra*:

> He has no need at all of anything that is made ... All things are by Him and for Him. He utters Himself also for His own delight and sees that he is good. He is His

---

[10] See generally Dolezal's *All That is in God*.

[11] Mike Ovey, 'Can we speak of "the" gospel in a postmodern world? Pluralism, polytheism and the gospel of the One, true God,' in *The Goldilocks Zone*, 193

[12] Ovey, 'Pluralism,' *The Goldilocks Zone*, 190.

[13] Graham Kendrick, 'Come and See' (Make Way Music, 1989).

own begotten and what proceeds from Him is Himself. Blessed be He![14]

This works in terms of his *attributes* and his *Trinitarian relations*. The Father is always Father, because he always has a Son. There is no point at which the Son appears and the Father becomes a Father. This is called *eternal generation*. The Son has always existed, he was not created by the Father. But the Son is also a Son, and not the Father. He is equal to the Father but different; God is three and God is one.

In the film, *Avengers Infinity War,* the villain Thanos seeks six infinity stones, which will give him the same status as God. These stones give him the power of:

Omnipresence (he can be anywhere – because of the Reality Stone, the Time Stone, and the Space Stone – yet he is still confined to one space at a time)

Omnipotence (all power – because of the Power Stone)

Omniscience (all knowledge – because of the Mind Stone)

Sovereignty (because of the Soul Stone)

Thanos must amass these stones (like parts) into one place and that *changes* him. We've seen this is not at all what God is like. God is different, God is perfect, God is simple. God does not share our limitations, precisely because he is different, perfect, and simple.

---

[14] C S Lewis, *The Space Trilogy* (Harper Collins, 2013), 337.

3. God is omnipresent (unlimited by time and space)

> 'I call all times soon,' said Aslan.
> *Voyage of the Dawn Treader*, C S Lewis

Have you ever wished you were in two places at once?

There is one part of space and time that we occupy, and we move along in sequence. We grow in knowledge, understanding and capability, and we never know what is around the corner – not one hundred per cent anyway.

God's Creator nature is perfect. For him to be perfect, that means he is not limited. He cannot be limited by anything outside of his perfect character. Here we ask: *where must God be to be the perfect promise keeper?*

The attribute of omnipresence means that God is not, never has been, and never will be limited by time or space. *He is everywhere, all at once, all the time.* There is nowhere that God is not. No one can hide from God. That is therefore the answer to our big question about where God must be to be the perfect promise keeper. But, as usual, it will need unpacking.

I am a big fan of *Doctor Who*. In this television series, the main character belongs to a race of aliens called Time Lords. They can travel in (but are still restricted by) time. To borrow from this concept, we might say that God is the ultimate Lord of Time. God controls time as the Creator of time. He is not controlled *by* time. He is never late nor early. For God, time is not linear as it is to us, because he is not restricted to being inside of it. For God, everything is *now*.[15]

---

[15] Rodgers, *Perfect Being Theology*, 57.

This is extremely confusing, and so we turn to Scripture for help in understanding it.

Look at these verses in Genesis 1, and ask yourself the question, where is God?

> In the beginning God created the heavens and the earth. Now the earth was formless and empty, darkness was over the surface of the deep, and the Spirit of God was hovering over the waters. And God said, 'Let there be light,' and there was light. God saw that the light was good, and he separated the light from the darkness. God called the light 'day', and the darkness he called 'night'. And there was evening, and there was morning – the first day. (Genesis 1:1–5)

Did you find him? Try the same with John 1:1–3

> In the beginning was the Word, and the Word was with God, and the Word was God. He was with God in the beginning. Through him all things were made; without him nothing was made that has been made.

Where is God?

Genesis 1 and 2 tell us that God made *everything*. That includes all of space: the entire span of the universe, everything that exists. It also includes time. The creation account shows days being made and divided up by the sun and moon which, interestingly, were created on the fourth day rather than at the start – time is made by

God. Therefore, to *make* it, he must be outside of it. To *control* it, he must be outside of it.

A comic strip tells a visual story. These pictures are divided into panels across the page. If there was enough space, we could see the span of one story, beginning to end, displayed on these panels, *because we are outside it*. For God to be the perfect promise keeper in Scripture, he must be unlimited in time and space.

4. God is omniscient (unlimited in wisdom, knowledge and goodness)

God's perfection and unimprovability also extends into the important area of knowledge. We believe and trust that God can and will keep his promises. Therefore, we are asking: *what must God know to be the perfect promise keeper?*

The Bible does not give us a list of everything God knows, for such a task is impossible. Instead, Scripture informs us *how* God knows, and from this we can correctly infer *what* he knows. Let us think back to Revelation 4:11:

> You are worthy, our Lord and God, to receive glory and honour and power,for you created all things,and by your will they were created and have their being.

Can you see what this passage is telling us? The whole created existence came from, and still exists by, the will of God. He is not a creator who creates and then sits back to watch. It is not the case of the proverbial blind watchmaker. The God of the Bible is not just

Creator of all, He is Sustainer of all. Nothing comes into existence, or continues to exist, outside the active will of God. Therefore, this directs us towards the extent and content of God's knowledge. His knowledge is unrestricted. In short, omniscience can be defined like this: *God knows everything about everyone all at the same time.*[16]

There is nothing that God does not know. We cannot have that knowledge as creatures, but God, as uncreated Creator, can and does. We are limited in our knowledge because we are bound by time and space – we do not know the future.

Our knowledge of the future is not perfect – and neither is our knowledge of the present. We do not know everything about ourselves. I do not know how many hairs I have, for example – just that the number decreases with each passing year. Our knowledge of the past is imperfect as well: I do not know what I did the second after I was born, and I don't know the names of my great-grandparents. We do not have perfect knowledge.

Furthermore, we do not begin with *any* knowledge. As infants, we have no knowledge of anything and we have to learn how to do all sorts of things. I remember my first week in a new job at a publishing company. There were many aspects of the role I had to learn, and quickly. As much as I would have loved to have been born knowing exactly how to do everything required, I was not. To do things, we need to learn how to do them.

However, when it comes to God, there is nothing that

---

16 I am grateful to Mike Ovey for this explanation.

he needs to learn. He literally knows everything, all the time, all at once. There is nothing he has gained that once he did not know, for that would mean there was an imperfection, something lacking in God. In other words, it would have made him improvable – better than he now is. Hebrews 4:12–13 says:

> For the word of God is alive and active. Sharper than any double-edged sword, it penetrates even to dividing soul and spirit, joints and marrow; it judges the thoughts and attitudes of the heart. Nothing in all creation is hidden from God's sight. Everything is uncovered and laid bare before the eyes of him to whom we must give account.

God's knowledge is *perfect* and without limit. He has no ignorance, or he would not be perfect. Nothing is hidden from him. His word, like a sword, penetrates beyond any barrier we throw in front of it. We cannot hide *anything* from him. This is a sobering fact that challenges our attempts to hide our imperfections. Even if we are seasoned practitioners at wearing our 'Sunday best,' or doing certain visible jobs, or smiling to hide how we really feel, nothing escapes the knowledge of God.

> Oh, the depth of the riches of the wisdom and knowledge of God! How unsearchable his judgments, and his paths beyond tracing out! 'Who has known the mind of the Lord? Or who has been his counsellor? Who has ever given to God, that God should repay them?' For from him and through him and for him are all things. To

> him be the glory for ever! Amen. (Romans 11:33–36)

God needs nothing from the outside: no council of advisers, no Google searches or Wikipedia articles. His knowledge is deeper than we can ever imagine. He knows everything about everything and everyone all at once. Losing *any* of that means losing *all* of it. That is our language of simplicity again.

We cannot lose any aspect of God. Because he is simple and not complex. To lose any aspect of God would mean losing all. And he would no longer be the perfect promise keeper in Scripture.

God's knowledge is not like ours. He does not observe processes and note down things for the future. For him, knowledge is a simple, single act. God does not grow in knowledge like we do – he knows everything already. Consider the following: if all we have said about God and his knowledge *wasn't* true, what would be the impact on this verse from Genesis 50?

> You intended to harm me, but God intended it for good to accomplish what is now being done: the saving of many lives. (Genesis 50:20)

This is at the end of the story of Joseph. To give context, Joseph has been sold into slavery, sent to a land far away from home, and later imprisoned for a crime he did not commit. But now, he is second in command of Egypt and has reconciled with his brothers who sold him in the first place.

Is this a happy accident or pure luck? Not according to

Joseph. He says that not only did God know what was coming, he *planned* what was coming to bring about his right purposes. It was not Plan B. What other way could we understand this verse than recognising that God is omniscient? It is worth remembering this truth, because a lot of people will disagree.

Rodgers puts it succinctly: 'Knowledge is good. So, a Perfect Being must have the most possible knowledge in the best possible way.'[17]

5. God is omnipotent (unlimited in power)

> '...he seems to be at the back of all the stories.'
> *The Horse and His Boy*, C S Lewis

God is the perfect promise keeper in Scripture. *Therefore*, he is unimprovable. *Therefore*, he is unlimited in:

- Where he is – he is *everywhere* all at once
- What he knows – he knows *everything* about everyone all at once

Without these truths in place, he cannot keep his promises perfectly. There is still more to consider though. Yes, we have established he is everywhere and knows everything, but is God just a bystander? We now ask: *what must God be able to do, to keep his promises perfectly?*

Once more, we begin with our headline answer as attested to by Scripture: *God is all powerful*. There is no being that can match him. He is above and beyond any superhero, or indeed, any world leader, body builder or

---

17 Rodgers, *Perfect Being Theology*, 71.

weapon wielder. Rodgers again:

> As the absolute creator of the world out of nothing he is the source of all being and hence of all powers and abilities possessed by his creations. Whatever anything is able to do, it is able to do it because it is immediately sustained right now by God.[18]

God is Creator and Sustainer. He does not sit and watch, knowing – or merely hoping – that his promises will be kept. God is not just someone who has access to every spoiler alert. If Disney got in touch with me and told me exactly what was going to happen in the next *Star Wars* film, then I would have foreknowledge, but nothing more. I would not be able to *influence* the course of action in these films. I would just be aware of what was going to happen.

If God is a foreknower alone, then he cannot be a perfect promise keeper. Because how can he ensure these promises will happen? He does not just *know* his promises will happen; he *actively keeps them*, because he is powerful enough to keep them.

A quick read through Mark's Gospel finds the power that Jesus, God the Son, demonstrates: he displays power over people, sickness, the weather, death, teaching and – biggest of all – he displays his power to forgive sins and raise from the dead. A children's song exemplifies this with the repeated refrain, 'Only God can do that!'[19]

---

18 Rodgers, *Perfect Being Theology*, 92.
19 Paul Sheely, 'Who Is This Man?' (Emu Music Australia, Inc, 1998).

None of those passages could be true if God were not all powerful. Indeed, Mark's purpose in recording these events is to demonstrate the claims of Christ, and his power to save everyone who believes. However, this leads us into a very common objection about the perfection of God. The uncomfortable logic goes something like this:

If God is all powerful, all knowing, all good and everywhere, why doesn't he stop suffering?

The answer cannot be said quickly. Christopher Ash approaches this question in two ways.[20] There is, first, the *armchair* question. This term means that people are discussing this question in theory, while generally having an easy life. The second is the *wheelchair* question. This means that people are being forced to answer this question because all sorts of horrible things have happened or are happening. They are forced to confront the question of why. As I've said, depression dogs me. I have wanted answers to this question many times – and I keep needing to have it answered.

Three common answers to this conundrum have developed:

- God *cannot stop* suffering. Otherwise, he would have done so, because that is *good*.
- God *did not know* the suffering was coming. Otherwise, he would have stopped it, because that is *good*.
- God *will not stop* the suffering, so he is *not good*.

As you consider these options, take time to think about

---

[20] Christopher Ash, *Job: The Wisdom of the Cross* (Preaching the Word) (Wheaton, IL: Crossway, 2014), 18ff.

their implications. Are any of them true? Would you use any of them to try and solve the problem? Where would that leave God's status as perfect promise keeper?

Let us make this more real. Go back over the three options and replace the word 'suffering' with whatever is your biggest worry. (For me, it is depression.) How do they sound now? Are they enough? Where do they leave us?

I want to say, and I hope you agree, that none of these three is true, and that is a relief. We have seen that God *can* stop suffering, that he *cannot* be surprised because he knows everything, and that he is *all good*. So where does that leave us?

It means that *any* suffering that happens, happens *inside* God's control.

Therefore, if he lets it happen, it can only be for his good purpose.

Otherwise, he would not let it happen.

This can be difficult to understand – not from an intellectual position, but an emotional one, especially as suffering is so hard to bear. 'My son's death is good then, is it?!' cried someone in the street at a friend of mine. 'If there is a God why would I have a brain tumour?!' objected another person I spoke to.

We do not want to diminish that suffering. We do not want to develop a formula that dismisses the real pain of these people. Suffering is hard. It is an inevitable, yet heart-breaking consequence of living in a fallen world. This does not mean that justice will not be done on wrong-doers. Nor does it mean that we are not allowed to express our sadness or anger in our suffering. In other words, God's good plan does not mean we have to pretend to be happy. Far from it. As we will find in the Psalms, Ecclesiastes or Job, God gives us the emotional language to help us in hard times.

I am a Christian – and I suffer from clinical depression. I am a minister and my first year as a vicar was one of almost utter misery. I love children but I cannot have any of my own. I was brought up in an emotionally abusive environment – and that affects me every day.

I do not list my woes for sympathy or attention. I do so merely to put aside any thought that I might be into just theory and not practice. The goodness of God has been a question – or a tear-induced rant – for me. Many times.

God is not vindictive. He permits what he could prevent, and he prevents what he could permit, *if* they are part of his perfect promise-keeping purpose. The implication is that if suffering happens, it is *only* so that God's good plan may actively continue, even though we may not recognise that. Remember, we are *creatures*, and he is *Creator*.

Let me give you another example. Back in January 2017, Mike Ovey – who was my college principal and the man responsible for much of the content of this book – died suddenly. He was a good man. He was a loving and caring husband and father, he had a phenomenal brain, a passion for the truth about God, a passion for teaching people like me how to teach God's truth and was someone who cared for his students. To my mind, his humour is unmatched. He was remarkable in many ways. Therefore, the question comes: why? Why take our best player off the pitch, at half time, before the game is over, without a confident lead on goal difference? I do not know the answer to this, but what I know about the perfection of God, and the Creator-Creature distinction – both of which Mike taught me – continues to be of immense comfort and hope.

If we step into Scripture, we will discover that Job is a big help with this. This is because he suffered more than any of us could imagine. He suffered not because he had done anything wrong, but because, as we are told at the start of the book, Satan stated that Job only worshipped God because he had a good life. This contrasts with God's statement of Job's faithfulness. Satan accused God of lying, and that cannot be. So, God let Satan attack Job to vindicate his own truth. The suffering that God let happen to Job proved that God is worthy of worship in and of himself. Satan's accusation that Job was only a 'fair weather' worshipper is proved utterly false. Instead, we find that, even when life gets unbearably hard, Job remains steadfast. It is God's glory that matters most – however hard that may be for me to remember as I cry frustrated tears when things are difficult.

This is not meant to be a glib answer. There are times when there are visible explanations as to why suffering was permitted, or the good prevented. But we do not always have that luxury. However, there is still an anchor of hope. We may not find out *why* certain things happen to us. But we do know that God is all powerful. Suffering happens for a reason, and God speaks to us through it and in it. We are forged in the valley of suffering before we can ascend the mountain of joy. That is the pattern of God the Son, Jesus Christ: suffering first, followed by resurrection and glory. If any wish to follow him, we must walk his footsteps – the way of the cross, with the cost of discipleship. That pattern is: suffering now, glory later. Jesus was not spared that – and neither are we. Suffering isn't surprising to God, or to us. And suffering does not ever compromise his goodness. I state this, not to sound uncaring, but because we need to remember it when suffering comes. All too often, this truth flies out of my brain as if I'd fired it out with a cannon.

6. *God is immutable (he cannot change)*

God's creator-ly perfection means he is unimprovable. Therefore, he does not change. He is the same yesterday, today and forever. He is outside of time and space. Therefore, he does not change like we do. He cannot grow up or grow old. He is always the same. He is not created, he is the Creator. So, God is not subject to 'being in the right mood' and he doesn't change his mind. God *never* changes his mind. He does not change.

If God was subject to change, if he was prone to changing his mind, how could we trust him?

However, some might say that there are instances in the Bible where God appears to change his mind or regret or reverse a decision he has made. An obvious example is found in the book of Jonah. At the start of the book, God says he will destroy Nineveh. By the end of the book, he does not destroy them – apparently in response to the people's repentance.

What do we make of this? A surface reading suggests that God has changed his mind. If we take this verse out of context, then we might possibly make a case for saying that. However, ripping verses from their context risks making Scripture say something it does not. If we say that God must have changed his mind, we limit him and deny his perfection. We also fail to consider what other parts of Scripture tell us about his character and his ways. Article 20 of the Thirty-Nine Articles is extremely helpful for us at this point:

> It is not lawful for the Church to ordain any thing that is contrary to God's Word written, neither may it so expound one place of Scripture, that it be repugnant to another.

In other words, we cannot interpret certain verses of Scripture in a way that makes them contradictory to others. A good understanding of the doctrine of God is a helpful safeguard for us on this point. If we have the doctrine of immutability in place, it will help us expound verses that may otherwise seem to be contradictory.

Therefore, this verse in Jonah does not tell us that God has changed his mind. For, it was always the plan! Notice, it is the *people* who have changed and not God. We know that – not just because of any outside doctrinal thought that has been imposed on the text, but because of what the text itself goes on to say. We know this cannot be God changing his mind from Jonah's angry outburst at the start of chapter 4:

> Isn't this what I said, Lord, when I was still at home? That is what I tried to forestall by fleeing to Tarshish. I knew that you are a

gracious and compassionate God, slow to anger and abounding in love, a God who relents from sending calamity.

Jonah knew all along that God would send him with a message of warning to the Ninevites, calling them to change. And Jonah knew it was always God's intention that the Ninevites should repent and that the plan to save them would ultimately happen. So he ran away.

God had not changed his plan. From our perspective, it seems that he did. However, from God's perspective, he did not. Here is a clear example of an *incommunicable* attribute being communicated. God is outside time, and we are not. While he is not subject to change, the only way we can see things is in sequential order, which gives an appearance of change. But, in reality, God did not react or change. This fact means that God can keep every promise perfectly. He will not change his mind. He will not change.

This applies to all aspects of God. Remembering our foundation of simplicity – he has not *gained* attributes, he has always had them.

7. *God is impassible (his feelings do not change)*

If any of God's attributes were to rub people up the wrong way, this would probably be top of the list. Impassibility, while often mis-defined as unfeeling, is actually an extension of immutability. God is not fickle, emotionally speaking. Many liberal theologians disagree with it.[21] And many conservative ones do too.[22] So where does impassibility fit in? This is asking the next big question: *what does God feel?*

To agree with impassibility is to agree that God's unchanging being includes his emotional state – in other words, that he does not change how he feels, as we do. Everything culminates here. God is everywhere; he knows everything and is all powerful. He is simple, not made up of bits. He does not feel as we do. He is not fickle. This does not mean God does not have emotions, but that God is not *moved* to an emotional feeling or reaction by us his creatures.

So, we can say that impassibility means this: *God, in himself, cannot suffer.* Because God's feelings do not change, he does not suffer (as a human might) when he sees people in situations of suffering. In fact, he *cannot* suffer because his feelings are not changed in reaction to what he sees.

Does this make you uneasy? I'll admit it does for me. Impassibility does not mean God is emotionless, and it does not deny the suffering of Jesus on the cross. It is saying God is not *moved* to react to us. In his outside-of-time-and-space, un-surprise-able nature, he cannot be moved to react in an un-perfect way. That is what we mean. And that, says Athanasius, for example, is why

---

[21] Clark Pinnock and Jürgen Moltmann would be big names here.
[22] For example, Tim Keller, John Stott, John Frame, Wayne Grudem and Don Carson – an intimidating list if you know those names! Those who argue in favour of impassibility include Mike Ovey, Garry Williams, James Dolezal and Thomas Weinandy.

Jesus became man – so that the God-Man could suffer as a human in our place.

God is God, and I am not. He is completely different from me and yet can still be known by me. He does not suffer like I do – he does not have fluctuating, reactive, fickle emotions, like I do. He cannot get weighed down like I can. He can keep his promises perfectly, *unlike* me. That is why I find the impassible God such good news. I do not need a God of empathy – I need a God of salvation.

To be fickle is to be changing frequently, especially as regards one's loyalties or affections. We are all like this to a certain extent. If God was like that, we would not be saved. If God didn't feel like keeping his promises, then there would be no rescue. If God got fed up with me failing again and again, I would have no chance. Nobody would ever have a chance with God, if he were fickle. Thankfully, he is not.

If God were 'passible' – in other words, subject to change of feelings, what would that do to his promises? If God were emotional and fickle, like we are, could he keep his promises perfectly? What if he, like me, did not 'feel' like keeping his promises? Does suffering limit God? I am afraid it does. As Rodgers concludes her section on this subject:

> Myself, I find the idea of a God who is made to suffer by us, and who needs us to be fulfilled, a depressing conception of divinity. In any case, it does not square with the other attributes of a perfect being, like simplicity and immutability. So if we are committed to perfect being theology

> we can safely trust that God experiences only infinite love and joy ... immutably.[23]

Passibility introduces blemishes and imperfections into the Godhead. If God is sad, then he needs improving.[24] Or if God *becomes* angry, then he is no longer immutable. We need our language of simplicity again. Because, if we follow the logic, emotional change makes God less perfect. Why? If God becomes sad, he changes and needs improving. Because he is simple, this applies to his whole being. His sadness would be an indication that he would need improving – and, therefore, he would not be perfect.

Does this mean God does not have feelings or emotions? No, it does not mean that at all. It is true to say there is emotional language ascribed to God in Scripture. But remember that we see this from our creaturely position: a communication of the incommunicable. It is true to say God is angry at our sin, sorrowful at our suffering and joyful in our salvation.

So, when we read passages such as Jonah 3 and 4, from our creaturely level, it looks like God has changed his mind. That is because we are in time, and so things are revealed progressively or sequentially. That is *our* perspective – but it does not mean it is what is actually going on. From our perspective, the sun seems to go up and down. But that is not what the sun is doing.

God is outside of time and immutable, and so his emotions do not fluctuate and change; for God is all

---

23 Rodgers, *Perfect Being Theology*, 53.
24 Hence the medieval position: 'it is better to be happy than sad, so God must be infinitely happy.' Rodgers, *Perfect Being Theology*, 51.

of his attributes at the same time. In affirming this, we are actually affirming a better story than one of passibility. If only the suffering God can help, we have empathy, but no action. We have a surprised God, on the backfoot, rather than the perfect promise keeper. For, if *only* empathy is what can be offered, where is the solution?

For example, when a tragic event hits the headlines, we are able to use social media, such as Facebook, to add badges or frames to our profile pictures in gestures of solidarity. I am not necessarily disagreeing with this practice but it does not equal a solution. It doesn't involve travelling to an area to help victims and offering them a *solution*. All we are doing, at best, is expressing sorrow in response to atrocity. At worst, we are virtue signalling.

If God is passible, then all he is able to do is change his profile picture. He is *reactive* to something, and that reaction is being moved to sorrow. There is no *solution*.

But the *impassible* God provides a *solution* to the problem behind suffering. A solution to our sin.

All this does not mean God doesn't *feel*, but it does mean that his feelings are perfect and that they do not change or fluctuate or react. God is not an emotionless Dalek, but a bundle of perfectly controlled and compatible emotions.

In terms of what does God feel, Garry Williams uses the term 'maximally alive' to describe any emotional state within the Divine being.[25] In response to our first objection that divine impassibility renders God a 'loveless stone,' he states: 'This is what God is like: he is not emotionally dead, but maximally sensitive to every tremor of his creation.'[26] Thomas Weinandy makes similar comments.[27]

For Williams, therefore, divine impassibility does not relegate God to indifference. Rather, it safeguards his perfect immutability. So, we need to define our terms. This is always an important exercise in explaining theology, and especially so here. There are, of course, two ways to suffer:

- *Voluntary suffering:* For example, voluntary suffering may arise from choosing to run a marathon. It is a painful exercise. It involves suffering (especially if you are as unfit as I am). However, it has not been forced upon you. It should not surprise you, because you have *chosen* to do it.

- *Involuntary suffering:* This is suffering you have no control over. For example, imagine you've finished your daily marathon training session at the gym. You go into the changing room where, to your surprise, you find a testosterone-driven fellow gym goer who decides to punch you in the face with no warning. That is going

---

25 Garry J. Williams, *His Love Endures Forever: Reflections on the Love of God* (Nottingham: IVP, 2015), 135. By this term, he means that God is at his maximum: his divine experience is complete, not limited.
26 Williams, *His Love Endures*, 129, 135.
27 Weinandy defines impassibility as God's inability to undergo an emotional change in state, which does not therefore mean he is passionless. See Thomas G. Weinandy, *Does God Suffer?* (Edinburgh: T&T Clark, 2000), 38–39.

to hurt. It causes you some form of suffering. You didn't choose this. It is painful, it takes you off guard.

In the light of what we have just seen, we must conclude that God can only suffer *voluntarily*. You cannot make God jump, you cannot leap out at him and shout 'Boo!' because he *already* knows that you are there, and always knew you were going to be there. Therefore, God cannot be surprised by suffering; he is not reactive, he is sovereign. If we affirm that God suffers *involuntarily*, we are in effect denying his complete sovereignty, because we are placing something outside of his control. It is easily shown, therefore, that to affirm involuntary suffering is to unravel much of the doctrine of God. So, our question now is not *can* God suffer? But in *what way* can God suffer?

In saying God can only suffer voluntarily, we are not saying that he is indifferent to our suffering. This is usually the charge levelled at those of us who confess impassibility. However, we are not calling God indifferent, but in charge. As we have noted, passibility is nothing more than an empathetic gesture, like adding a Facebook profile picture frame. We need more than that – we need God to solve the problem. Impassibility means God has a solution to the problem – and the problem isn't the suffering itself, but the sin behind it.

The incarnation of the Son of God is the solution to this dilemma. For, we can affirm that – yes, Jesus does suffer on the cross. It would be an insult and flat-out denial of Scripture to say otherwise. For example, we read in Isaiah 53:

> Surely he took up our pain and bore our suffering, yet we considered him punished by God, stricken by him, and afflicted. But he was pierced for our transgressions, he was crushed for our iniquities; the punishment that brought us peace was on him, and by his wounds we are healed. (Isaiah 53:3–4)

How can we say, 'God does not suffer' in light of the cross? The impassibility of God does not contradict the passibility of Jesus as he died on the cross. There is no contradiction. God the Father and God the Holy Spirit do not suffer on the cross. But nor is the Son ripped away from the Trinity. Christ suffers *voluntarily*, in his humanity, while retaining his divinity. Herein lies the mystery of the Trinity.

If God suffers involuntarily, then there is something that needs improving. We risk losing the biblical picture of God if we deny impassibility. Instead, we are left with a divine Eeyore. Our emphasis has become skewed. It is not that Christ shares in *our* sufferings that is important (though he knows what it is like to suffer, because of the incarnation), it is the warning from the lips of Jesus that we are to share in *his* sufferings:

> Whoever wants to be my disciple must deny themselves and take up their cross and follow me. For whoever wants to save their life will lose it, but whoever loses their life for me will find it. (Matthew 16:24–25)

Impassibility is part of God's unchanging nature.[28] It means that God *does not change in his emotions.*[29] But God the Son became incarnate and he *voluntarily* suffered on the cross for our redemption. Thus, God can keep his promises. Impassibility is not a philosophical import that makes God indifferent to suffering.[30] Nor does confessing it deny the Scriptural language of emotion ascribed to God.[31]

The perfect Father

We have noted many things about God in his perfection: he is simple (without parts), he is omnipresent (everywhere), omniscient (all knowing), omnipotent (all powerful), immutable (unchanging), impassible (without 'passions,' not subject to emotional change). But what do these huge concepts do in terms of our search for a perfect Father? Surely all these attributes do is make God feel even more alien than we first thought?

For me, it is quite the opposite. I need a God who is not like me. Any father, good or bad, is not perfect – they are limited. But God is perfect and his perfection is utterly beautiful and of deep assurance to us as believers. That assurance comes from the fact that we have a constant and consistent God. A God who never 'doesn't feel like' being God. A God who never gets fed up, overwhelmed, defeated, surprised or diminished.

---

28 This is the necessary conclusion we will reach in our doctrinal and scriptural analysis.

29 The word 'fickle' would be appropriate to use at this point. However, pastorally, I would want to be clear on the definition of that term, hence a reproduction of the meaning of the term, rather than the term itself.

30 John Stott, Tim Keller, Don Carson and others.

31 Clark Pinnock and Jürgen Moltmann, for example.

God's perfection is too high for me to give it proper justice – but it communicates such a perfection that I am wrapped into joy. This joy comes from knowing this God is for me and communicates to me as Father through the Son and Spirit.

God as Father

One God in three Persons

We have spent much time on how God is not like us. He is perfect and unimprovable. He does not, in himself, suffer and so he is our anchor of hope in the storms of life. By virtue of being Creator not creature, God is not limited in ways that we are. He is perfect and therefore keeps every promise perfectly. He is in every way the perfect Father we all long for – and need.

A book discussing the nature and character of God would not be complete without some reflection on the fact God is one God in three Persons. Most pertinent for our discussion is the fact God is Father. The idea of God as Father carries much baggage in our society. For all sorts of reasons, some people struggle with the idea of God being our Father. That may be because their own father fell very far short of their calling to father well, or because their much loved father is no longer with them, or because they are grappling with issues of gender and sexuality. It is, therefore, pertinent and precious when the desire for a perfect father is ultimately discovered in the God who is just that: a Perfect Father.

Despite issues that many of us have around the concept of fatherhood, I still believe that it is wonderful, pastorally, that God is our Father. Let us unpack what this means. The Bible calls God 'Father', because the Bible records the words of Jesus Christ. If we particularly note the way Jesus speaks of the Father in John's Gospel, this filial relationship is front and centre. Simply, God is a Father because he has a Son, Jesus

Christ. They are equal in substance and dignity, yet different in operation – in other words, in what they do.

The Fatherhood of God is part of God's Trinitarian nature. The Bible, though it does not use the word Trinity, clearly portrays that God is Triune: he is one God, in three Persons. He is not three gods, nor is he one being that changes or appears in different guises or 'modes'. This is perhaps the most complicated doctrine in Christian theology! I will not attempt a full explanation here – once again, it is beyond the scope of this work. But as we consider the pastoral implications of this doctrine, we note that the Trinity implies relationship. The reason why we can say God is love is because he is a Trinity. He knows how to have relationships, based on self-giving and other-person-centred love.

In so many ways, God is not like me – but, in this instance, I am like him because he is relational. Jesus himself points people to the Fatherhood of God, and to the relationships between all three members of the Trinity, as reassurance in times of worry. Of course, although Jesus is speaking to his disciples here, through eyes of faith, we join them around the supper table to listen in on this discourse that provides reassurance to us as disciples too. To see this, we turn to chapter 14 of John's Gospel.

Reassurance in times of worry

From chapter 13 to 17, John tells us all that goes on at the Last Supper – the final meal Jesus and his friends share together. In chapter 13, we see what cross-shaped love looks like as Jesus washes the disgusting feet of his disciples. It is a picture of the love that is demonstrated on the cross – a love for the unlovely, a love that is fundamentally self-giving and other-person-centred. We also hear that not only will Jesus be betrayed by someone round that table, but that even Peter will deny knowing him. It is no wonder then that the disciples are discouraged. Jesus is leaving them soon and they are worried about what they are going to do.

The person they have placed their hope in will be taken away, like a rug being snatched from under their feet. For someone with depression, this is a familiar feeling. They need a lot of comfort. And they *will* receive it. The comfort they will receive is very similar to what Job received: the comfort here is in who God is.

The comfort of a room in his Father's house (verses 1–6)

Jesus says to his friends: 'Do not let your hearts be troubled. Trust in God; trust also in me.' The first piece of comfort that Jesus offers his disciples is trusting Jesus when he says he's going to prepare a place for them in heaven. He says so in verse 2: 'In my Father's house are many rooms; if it were not so, I would have told you. I am going there to prepare a place for you.'

Jesus is returning to heaven via the cross, because that is how he washes people clean. He washes them by dirtying himself – by shedding his blood – so that he can wash us clean. All that we find out from Jesus here is that heaven is roomy. There is plenty of space – many rooms, like a mansion. And those rooms are reserved by Jesus for his people. There is a place in God's new creation which has our name on it – because Jesus said so.

Jesus goes on: 'And if I go and prepare a place for you, I will come back and take you to be with me that you also may be where I am.' Not only is he going to prepare a place for them, he is also going to come back and take them there himself. Now that's room service, is it not? Not only does he reserve the room, and not only does he get it ready, he promises to come back and take them there personally.

Depression can make you feel like you are out of reach of God's love. To extend the analogy of a house with many rooms, it can sometimes feel as if the reservation has been cancelled, because the depressed person cannot or will not pay any kind of deposit. But that misses the point. Depression does not rule out our reserved room, because God is God. The promise of a place in his house depends on him, not us. Whatever happens to us, however hard it gets, whatever makes us want to give up, please do not. Our state depends on God – and we have seen that he does not change.

So, the reserved sign is up, and it will never be taken down. Your name is on the door. Jesus tells his disciples that he is leaving them – but not forever. He goes on to explain that he will send his Holy Spirit to every believer, so they will never be alone. He, Jesus, will always somehow be with them, because God the Holy Spirit is with them. Believers are united with Christ, forever, awaiting his promised return. And that is how we live now, with depression as *part* of our lives – but not the *ruler*. These things are true because of God's nature.

Jesus takes the conversation on. Having been asked by Thomas how they should know the way, Jesus states: 'I am the way and the truth and the life. No one comes to the Father except through me.'

The disciples know the way. They might not *think* they do – but they do. And it does not depend on them. They are going to heaven and to the Father because they know Jesus – the way, the truth and the life.

God is relational, because he is one God in three Persons. Thus, this resurrection and future hope is guaranteed because it is based on relational promises made within the Godhead, rather than on anything we do or say. It does not depend on us! That is outstandingly beautiful, and it is all to do with God, not me.

Notice Jesus begins this statement with a strong: 'I am...' He makes a few statements like that in John's Gospel, and they're meant to grab our attention. This is because when Jesus says, 'I am', he is using the name God gives himself in the Old Testament. In Exodus 3, Moses encounters God in a bush on fire that doesn't burn up. He asks to know what name to give to the one who has spoken to Him. God says: 'I AM WHO I AM.'

God's name is what he does. As we have seen, the doctrine of simplicity reminds us God *is* his character. Remember the *Mr Men* and *Little Miss* books? God is what he does, just as the Mr Men and Little Miss characters do as their name says. Therefore, when Jesus says, 'I am,' he is reminding his disciples, and us that he is God himself, come down to humanity.

God comforts believers in distress with truth they can believe. He comforts them by reminding them of himself – and that is the best comfort anyone can ever hear. So, the disciples can be comforted – and so can we, because we know him. And because we know the Son, we know the Father. And because we know the Father and the Son, we have the Spirit. And therefore, we have life. We can sleep at night. We can keep going. We can be comforted – because Jesus is coming back to bring his people to the Father.

The comfort of a relationship with the Godhead (verse 7–14)

Jesus' words are not just the words of a special man. They come with authority – he is the divine Son. He speaks the words of his Father, for the Father is in him and he is in the Father. 'If you really knew me, you would know my Father as well. From now on, you do know him and have seen him' (verse 7). Jesus is claiming that the disciples know God the Father, *because* they know him, Jesus. They have seen the Father and know him, *because* they have seen and know Jesus. 'Whoever has seen me has seen the Father [...] Do you not believe that I am in the Father and the Father is in me?' (verse 9-10).

God is one in nature, three in Persons. He is one in being and one in purpose. Furthermore, he is three in persons and three in works for that one purpose. Thus, when the disciples see Jesus, they see the Father – one shows us the other. God wants us to share in the love the Father has for the Son. So, he sends Jesus who is in the Father.

When we meet Jesus in the pages of his Word by his Spirit, we are drawn into the everlasting, loving relationship between the Father and the Son and the Spirit. We are united with Jesus, by his Spirit. In other words, we are stuck to him, because he has stuck himself to us. We become God's child, and we are brought into relationship with God, and can call God 'Father' – that same God we have seen is different, perfect and simple, and much bigger than we could dream. We can call him 'Father' in the most intimate and secure relationship.

Therefore, for those in depression, or facing anxiety and worry, or grieving a damaging relationship with their earthly father, we are not alone in this fight. This is important, because these are isolating conditions. They either make one *feel* alone – or, sadly, in some cases, end up ostracising us from our social circles – either through others feeling like they do not know what to say, or that they are ill at ease.

God is relational, like me. Yet God is perfect, *not* like me. Therefore, the way he relates to me is never, ever compromised. He does not ever get fed up with me or fall out with me. Even though I am a bad friend – indeed, a bad son towards God – he will never return like for like. I can sleep at night, and keep going, because I am united with Jesus.

We have spoken a lot about the otherness of God – and quite rightly. He is thrice holy. He is the Creator whom I can only know by him lisping to me. But we can also say of this God who is 'other': he's my Dad.

This powerful, Perfect Being knows me, and loves me, as a father loves his child. Not all of us have enjoyed good, stable, comforting relationships with our fathers – and that does impact what we think about God as Father. My relationship with my dad hasn't been brilliant. I've lived trying to please him and failed, because we're so very different. That affects how I relate to God. I often lapse into thinking I must earn his love by trying to please him. A lot of my depression comes from that. Whatever our relationship with our dads, don't let that cloud this – even the best earthly dad is still a pale reflection of our heavenly Father who *never* messes up. If you know Jesus, you know the Father.

The mathematics of this passage goes like this:

> Knowing the Son = knowing the Father = knowing life

We and the disciples do know him, and so we have life. That is the comfort Jesus gives them as he goes to the cross. Because they know him, they know the Father. Therefore, they can trust him. Believe me, he says to the disciples. They can believe his words, and his work. They have seen them. The disciples can trust Jesus because they truly know him.

Therefore, they can pray along with his plan. He promises this in verses 13–14: 'And I will do whatever you ask in my name, so that the Father may be glorified in the Son. You may ask me for anything in my name, and I will do it.'

God is not Santa Claus – he does not give us our wish list based on how good our faith is. God will answer the disciples' prayers. And notice what else Jesus says: 'so that the Father may be glorified in the Son.' This reminds us of what we've seen: God does not give us instant relief from pain, unless it is part of his plan, for his glory and our good. The disciples know Jesus, *relationally* – and they have life because of that. Therefore, they can be comforted.

'Do not let your hearts be troubled,' Jesus says, because he is going to prepare a place for them in heaven by dying in their place on the cross and rising again to go to the Father. This is because of who he is – he is God, he is in the Father and he brings us into that relationship. There is such precious hope for the Christian – and even more for the Christian with depression or other troubles! Considering all the awesome, majestic perfection of God, we know him, like a dad. We know him as Father because we know Jesus. Thus, we are not alone in this fight. In my depression, I am comforted that I know him and that I am united with him. Because of that, I know the Father, and therefore, I know where I'm going. Knowing our destination helps our journey.

I love this quote from the fiftieth anniversary episode of *Doctor Who*: 'My journey is the same as yours, the same as anyone's. It has taken me so many years, so many lifetimes, but at last I know where I am going. Where I have always been going. Home. The long way round.'[1]

The Christian life is a bit like that anyway, even without being depressed. It is easy to forget where we are going, and it is easy to get bogged down in the inevitable mess of life, is it not? It is easy to feel overwhelmed, tired or fed up. There is not enough energy to get to church sometimes, or to make an effort to chat to people. Things naturally frustrate, tire and upset us, and so our journey plan is clouded. I need to remember this, as I lie awake at night, and sometimes, honestly, feel like giving up on a few things.

But this is the objective truth I want to speak into my

---

[1] Steven Moffat, 2013, 'The Name of the Doctor', *Doctor Who* (Wolf Studios, BBC).

subjective mess:

- Jesus has gone to prepare a room for us with his Father.
- Jesus is in his Father, so we know God adequately.
- We are utterly secure.
- We are united with Christ, by his Spirit, to his Father.
- We are going home.
- Our room is ready and waiting.
- Therefore, we can sleep at night and keep going, hard as it may be.

When your head hits your pillow tonight, remind yourself of your secure status and your reserved room. 'Do not let your hearts be troubled. Trust in God; trust also in me.'

Final Reflection: Will I Let God Disagree With Me?

> 'Aslan,' said Lucy, 'you're bigger.'
> 'That is because you are older,
> little one.'
> *Prince Caspian*, C S Lewis

It is impossible to put into words how magnificent our God is.[1] He has revealed enough of himself so that we may know him like Goldilocks knew that third bowl of porridge: just right.

What was your picture of God when you started out? Has anything been confirmed or changed? Why not write down the biggest thing you have learnt? I hope your view of God has grown, because there is always room for growth when it comes to the doctrine of God.

The book of Micah opens with an astoundingly huge vision of God – as the one who both judges and shows compassion to sinners:

> Hear, you peoples, all of you,
> listen, earth, and all who live in it,
> that the Sovereign LORD may bear witness against you,
> the Lord from his holy temple.
> Look! The LORD is coming from his dwelling-place;
> he comes down and treads on the heights of the earth.
> The mountains melt beneath him

---

[1] I am grateful to Robbie Strachan, in his chapel meditation at Oak Hill college on 11 September 2017, for these reflections.

> and the valleys split apart,
> like wax before the fire,
> like water rushing down a slope.
> (Micah 1:2–4)

This is a terrifying picture of an awesome God. It is also a picture of the God who saves, by keeping every promise perfectly. See how Micah bookends his work by returning to the God he proclaims:

> Who is a God like you,
> who pardons sin and forgives
> the transgression
> of the remnant of his inheritance?
> You do not stay angry forever
> but delight to show mercy.
> You will again have compassion on us;
> you will tread our sins underfoot
> and hurl all our iniquities into the depths
> of the sea.
> You will be faithful to Jacob,
> and show love to Abraham,
> as you pledged on oath to our ancestors
> in days long ago.
> (Micah 7:18–20)

Note the power and mercy of this awesome God, and especially note that final refrain: it is faithfulness to God's oaths, or promises, that is the source of our assurance of God's compassion.

Having looked at aspects of the doctrine of God, we end with a big question: *Is there space for Micah's kind of God?*

Micah's name means 'Who is like Yahweh?' Who is

like God? I hope we have seen that as perfect promise keeper, he is incomparable. Words fail us as we dwell on the majesty of God. So, what will you do with what you know?

It is not enough – though it is possibly a good start – to come away with greater knowledge of God. But, as Mike Ovey used to say, 'Good theology leads to doxology.' In other words, what we know will impact how we worship, which is how we live.

Perhaps our view of God is or was very different from what we have seen in this book. Sometimes when people come up against doctrine they don't like, they go looking for truth in other places, as Paul warns Timothy, 'For the time will come when people will not put up with sound doctrine. Instead, to suit their own desires, they will gather around them a great number of teachers to say what their itching ears want to hear' (2 Timothy 4:3).

Will I let God disagree with me? In other words, will I let the doctrine of God as revealed in Scripture *change* what I think? Or will I try and slot it into *my* worldview? Consider what we have learnt: are there any places where we need to let God disagree with us? Finally, are there any places where your big view of God needs to fill the gaps of sadness? For me, the study of the doctrine of God has helped fulfil a longing: searching for a perfect Father that I can only have in relationship with our one Triune God. And so, I leave you with the wonderful words of C S Lewis:

> Both the children were looking up into the Lion's face as he spoke these words. And all at once (they never knew exactly how it

happened) the face seemed to be a sea of tossing gold in which they were floating, and such a sweetness and power rolled about them and over them and entered them that they felt they had never really been happy or wise or good, or even alive and awake, before. And the memory of that moment stayed with them always, so that as long as they both lived, if ever they were sad or afraid or angry, the thought of all that golden goodness, and the feeling that it was still there, quite close, just round some corner or just behind some door, would come back and make them sure, deep down inside, that all was well.[2]

---

[2] C S Lewis, *The Magician's Nephew* in *The Chronicles of Narnia* (Harper Collins, 2001), 102–103.

Permissions

Latimer Trust are grateful for the following permissions:

Scripture quotations are taken from the New International Version UK (NIVUK). Holy Bible, New International Version® Anglicized, NIV® Copyright © 1979, 1984, 2011 by Biblica, Inc.® Used by permission. All rights reserved worldwide.

Perelandra by C.S. Lewis copyright © 1944 C.S. Lewis Pte. Ltd.

The Voyage of the Dawn Treader by C.S. Lewis copyright © 1952 C.S. Lewis Pte. Ltd.

The Horse and His Boy by C.S. Lewis copyright © 1954 C.S. Lewis Pte. Ltd.

Prince Caspian by C.S. Lewis copyright © 1951 C.S. Lewis Pte. Ltd.

The Magician's Nephew by C.S. Lewis copyright © 1955 C.S. Lewis Pte. Ltd.

Extracts reprinted by permission.

For further reading

On the doctrine of God

Athanasius of Alexandria. *On the Incarnation*. London: Amazon, 2012.

Augustine of Hippo. *Concerning the City of God against the Pagans*. Translated by Henry Bettenson. London: Penguin Classics, 2003.

Bavinck, Herman. *The Doctrine of God*. Translated by William Hendricksen. Edinburgh: Banner of Truth, 1977.

Bavinck, Herman. *Reformed Dogmatics Volume Two: God and Creation*. Translated by John Vriend. Edited by John Bolt. Grand Rapids: MI.: Baker Academic, 2004.

Beeke, Joel R and Mark Jones. *A Puritan Theology: Doctrine for Life*. Grand Rapids, MI: Reformation Heritage Books, 2012.

Bray, Gerald. *The Doctrine of God: Contours of Christian Theology*. Downers Grove, IL: Inter-Varsity Press, 1993.

Calvin, John. *Institutes of the Christian Religion*. Translated by Ford Lewis Battles. Edited by John T. McNeill. 2 vols. Lexington, KY: Westminster John Knox Press, 1960.

Carson, Don. *The Difficult Doctrine of the Love of God*. Nottingham: IVP, 2000.

Dolezal, James E. *All That is in God: Evangelical Theology and the Challenge of Classic Christian Theism*. Grand Rapids, MI.: Reformed Heritage Books, 2017.

Edgar, Brian. *The Bible Speaks Today: The Message of the Trinity*. Leicester: IVP, 2004.

Frame, John M. *A Theology of Lordship Volume 2: The Doctrine of God*. Phillipsburg, NJ: P&R Publishing, 2002.

Frame, John M. *Systematic Theology: An Introduction to Christian Belief*. Phillipsburg, NJ: P&R Publishing, 2013.

Hilary of Poitiers. *De Trinitate: On the Trinity*. Edited by Paul A. Boer Sr. Winona, TX: Veritatis Splendor Publications, 2012.

Horton, Michael. *The Christian Faith: A Systematic Theology for Pilgrims on the Way*. Grand Rapids, MI: Zondervan, 2011.

Hughes, R. Kent. *John: That You May Believe* (Preaching the Word Series). Wheaton, IL: Crossway, 1999.

Exposition of the Orthodox Faith by John of Damascus. *Church Fathers*. Kindle Locations 576609–576612.

Letham, Robert. *The Holy Trinity: In Scripture, History, Theology and Worship*. Phillipsburg, NJ: P&R Publishing, 2004.

Lister, Rob. *Impassible and Impassioned: Towards A Theology of Divine Emotion*. Wheaton, IL.: Crossway, 2013.

Ovey, Michael J. 'Is God the Only Theologian? "True but not Exhaustive."' Pages 37–51 in *Serving the Church Reaching the World: Essays in honour of Don Carson*. Edited by Richard Cunningham. London: IVP, 2017

Ovey, Michael J. *The Goldilocks Zone: Collected Writings of Michael J. Ovey*. Edited by Chris Green. Nottingham: IVP, 2018.

Ovey, Michael J. *Your Will Be Done: Exploring Eternal Subordination, Divine Monarchy and Divine Humility*. London: Latimer Trust, 2016.

Packer, J. I. *Concise Theology: A Guide to Historic Christian Beliefs*. Nottingham: IVP, 1993.

Rodgers, Katherin. *Perfect Being Theology*. Edinburgh: Edinburgh University Press, 2000.

Vos, Gerhaudus. *Reformed Dogmatics Vol 1: Theology Proper*. Translated by Richard B. Gaffin Jr. Bellingham, WA: Letham Press, 2014.

Weinandy, Thomas. *Does God Suffer?* Edinburgh: T&T Clark, 2000.

Williams, Garry, *His Love Endures Forever: Reflections on the Love of God*. Nottingham: IVP, 2015.

Young, William P. *The Shack: Where Tragedy Confronts Eternity*. London: Hodder and Stoughton, 2007.

On suffering

Ash, Christopher. *Preaching the Word: Job: The Wisdom of the Cross*. Wheaton, IL: Crossway, 2014.

Carson, D. A. *How Long O Lord? Reflections on Suffering and Evil* (Second Edition). Nottingham: Inter-Varsity Press, 2006.

Collins, Sarah and Jayne Haynes. *Dealing with Depression: Trusting God through the Dark Times*. Tain: Christian Focus Publications, 2011.

Cranmer, Thomas. *The Book of Common Prayer 1662*. Cambridge: Cambridge University Press.

Grimmond, Paul. *Suffering Well*. Kingsford: Matthias Media, 2011.

Lane, Tim. *Living Without Worry: How to Replace Anxiety with Peace*. London: The Good Book Company, 2015.

Lane, Timothy S. and Paul David Tripp. *How People Change*. Greensboro, NC: New Growth Press, 2008.

Lloyd-Jones, Dr Martyn. *Spiritual Depression: Its Causes and Cure*. Glasgow: Pickering and Inglis, 1965.

Tripp, Paul David. *Instruments in the Redeemer's Hands: People in Need of Change Helping People in Need of Change*. Phillipsburg, NJ: P&R Publishing, 2002.

Welch, Edward T. *Depression: Looking up from the Stubborn Darkness*. Greensboro, NC: New Growth Press, 2011.

Welch, Edward T. *When People are Big and God is Small: Overcoming Peer Pressure, Codependency and the Fear of Man*. Phillipsburg, NJ: P&R Publishing, 1997.

Also in our Christian Doctrine series

Those authorised to minister in the Church of England, whether as ordained or lay ministers, are expected to teach and act in accordance with the Church of England's doctrine. However, many of those who are currently exercising ministry in the Church of England, or who are being trained for ministry, are unclear about what the Church of England's doctrine is, and why it matters that they should adhere to it.

In order to address this situation, the Latimer Trust is producing a new series of short books on doctrine which are designed to introduce various key aspects of the doctrine of the Church of England. The purpose of *Deep Roots* is to introduce the series as a whole. It does this by explaining what doctrine is, the nature of the doctrinal authorities accepted by the Church of England, and why it is important for both ministers (and Christians in general) to adhere to what is taught by these doctrinal authorities.

This is a book for existing ministers, those in training for ministry and ordinary lay Christians who want a concise but reliable answer to the question 'What is doctrine and why does it matter?'

In our NEW Christian Leadership series

Bishops: A Concise Study summarises the key points of the argument of Martin's major study *Bishops Past, Present and Future* (Gilead Books 2022). It is designed to meet the needs of those who would like to know about the role and importance of bishops in the Church of England, but who would baulk at tackling the 800+ pages of the original book.

This concise study is published in the hope that it will help many in the Church of England, both ordained and lay, to think in a more informed fashion about how bishops should respond to the challenges and opportunities facing the Church of England at this critical point in its history.

Anglican polity has traditionally favoured the incumbent as sole elder over a congregation. Biblical and missional imperatives press for eldership to be plural but how can this be done within an Anglican setting?

This study explores the biblical and historical background to plural eldership or locally shared pastoral leadership. It goes on to describe the experience of nine UK Anglican pastors who have established a team that functions as a plural eldership. While the focus is on the church's ministry of making disciples, lessons are drawn for other areas of pastoral leadership.

The revised and expanded edition includes additional chapters on the role of women and on the place of power in pastoral ministry.

www.ingramcontent.com/pod-product-compliance
Lightning Source LLC
Chambersburg PA
CBHW031458040426
42444CB00007B/1141